BEGINNERS QUICK GUIDE
TO PASSIVE INCOME

Learn Proven Ways to Earn Extra Income in the Cyber World

Alex Nkenchor Uwajeh

Beginners Quick Guide to Passive Income:

Learn Proven Ways to Earn Extra Income in the Cyber World

By

Alex Nkenchor Uwajeh

Legal Disclaimers & Copyright Information

This book is presented to you for informational purposes only and is not a substitution for any professional advice. The contents herein are based on the views and opinions of the author and all associated contributors.

While every effort has been made by the author and all associated contributors to present accurate and up to date information within this document, it is apparent technologies rapidly change. Therefore, the

author and all associated contributors reserve the right to update the contents and information provided herein as these changes progress. The author and/or all associated contributors take no responsibility for any errors or omissions if such discrepancies exist within this document.

The author and all other contributors accept no responsibility for any consequential actions taken, whether monetary, legal, or otherwise, by any and all readers of the materials provided. It is the reader's sole responsibility to seek professional advice before taking any action on their part.

Reader's results will vary based on their skill level and individual perception of the contents herein, and thus no guarantees, monetarily or otherwise, can be made accurately, therefore, no guarantees are made.

CONTENTS

Introduction **7**

Blogging **10**

Monetizing Your Blogs **16**

Affiliate Marketing **20**

Sell Advertising **24**

Membership Sites **26**

Buying and Selling Websites **29**
    1 - Revamp Existing Websites 30
    2 - Outsource the Process 30
    3 - Generate Traffic and Revenue 31
    4 - Selling Websites for Profit 32

E-Mail Marketing 34

Information Products 38
    Selling Your Information Products 41

Write and Publish Books 44

Create and Sell Apps......................................49

Flipping Apps for Profit.............................50

Making Money from Free Apps 51

Offer Freelance Services Online 54

Create or Teach an Online Course 57

YouTube Videos 60

Selling Stock Photography 63

Invest in Stocks 66

Conclusion 70

INTRODUCTION

Did you know the internet is responsible for making more millionaires than any other medium in history?

If you're able to earn an income using a laptop computer and an internet connection, it becomes possible to make money from anywhere in the world.

The ability to earn extra income online gives you the opportunity to supplement the paycheck you get from your day job. You can use that additional cash to pay off debts, invest in new opportunities, take that long-overdue vacation, or just buy the things you want.

If you're serious, it's also possible to grow your online income to the point where it totally replaces the income you get from your day job.

Building a solid online business that generates revenue for you can be extremely lucrative, if it's done correctly. In fact, there are so many different ways to earn income online that you have the freedom to create your business around those options that suit you best.

Perhaps the biggest benefit to generating an income online is that you have the freedom to create multiple streams of income from your efforts. There's also the ability to create passive income streams, where you keep getting paid for your efforts long after you've done the initial work of setting it all up.

If you're like most people, you'll be ready to jump online and get started. Unfortunately, just like most other new online entrepreneurs, it can be hard to know which opportunities will work for you and which ones are a waste of your time and effort.

A quick search on any major search engine for 'making money online' will return millions of

results. Sure, you might earn a few cents from some of those opportunities, but earning a couple of bucks isn't the same thing as creating a real, sustainable income that can help you achieve financial freedom.

That's why this book was created. The opportunities outlined in this book give you some insight into some highly effective ways to generate real income streams. You'll find this book includes only proven methods for making money online.

Are you ready to get started? Let's go...

BLOGGING

Did you know there are people out there making six figure incomes each year from just blogging? It's true.

People all over the world are discovering ways to generate income from their blogs.

Anyone can set up a blog in just a few minutes with platforms like WordPress, Blogger and Typepad. Once your blog is up and running, you're live online and ready to write about whatever you want.

Serious bloggers command a massive following of people willing to read whatever they post on their blogs. In order to generate such a healthy income from blogging, those bloggers find effective ways to monetize each post.

The beauty of blogging platforms is that they're so easy to customize. You have the freedom to add simple banners and widgets to your blog that could help you generate income.

For example, you might decide to add a Google Adsense widget in the sidebar of your blog that shows ads right alongside each of your posts. You might add some banner advertising that links to an affiliate product related to your post's topic. There are plenty of monetization options available for your blogs and we'll go through many of them within this book.

Creating your blog and finding ways to generate money are a great start. However, your efforts won't do you any good if no one knows your blog exists. The real key to making money with your blog is to find ways to attract good quality visitors, and then match those visitors with pertinent income generation methods that match their needs.

Ideally, you want to attract people who have an interest in what you're writing about. Those people already want to learn more about your topic, so they're likely to become loyal followers. They're also the people who are far more likely to be interested in any products or services or advertisements related to your topic, which is how you generate income.

You can encourage people to your blogs by linking to your posts from your social media accounts, such as Facebook, Twitter, Google+, LinkedIn, or Pinterest. Any connections or groups or followers you have on those sites will see your posts and click over to view what you've written.

If you add social media sharing buttons or icons to the bottom of each post, you'll find some of your blog's visitors will share your posts around in their own circles, effectively increasing the amount of exposure you get to each post.

Incorporate good photos or high quality infographics or videos into your blog posts, as visual media has a much higher chance of going viral, or being shared among other circles.

Another way to attract good quality visitors is to write blog posts that offer more information on your chosen topic. After all, people search the internet for good information relating to their own interests. If your blog contains lots of helpful content that people find useful, informative, educational, or entertaining, you have a much better chance of turning your blogging efforts into a healthy stream of income.

Your content could include reviews of various products. You could simply write about your experiences or your knowledge of how to do things related to your topic. Your blog posts might be your way of keeping people informed about your progress while you learn more about a particular topic.

The whole key to success with blogging for money is to be consistent about posting regularly. It's not necessary to post something every day, but publishing something new to your blog once or twice a week is a good way to keep followers interested.

Most blogging platforms give you the ability to schedule your posts to be published on a specified day and time. This means you can write several blog posts at once and schedule them to be released a week apart.

If you're short on time, scheduling your blogging activities means you only need to spend a day a month creating your content, and then they're released automatically at regular intervals, leaving you free to work on other things.

MONETIZING
YOUR BLOGS

Building a popular blog might gain you some visitors and some recognition within your niche. However, you won't earn much unless you find realistic ways to monetize your efforts.

There are multiple ways to earn money from your blogs and some options will definitely be better than others. However, it's important to remember that different niches may see better results than others with some ad networks, while others may be better suited to different types of monetization programs.

The key is to mix and match your options until you find a combination that works for you to maximize your earnings.

Perhaps the most well-known option for many bloggers is Google Adsense. Most of us are

familiar with the Google advertising blocks available on some blogs. Each time a visitor clicks on one of those ads, you get paid. This is commonly known as Pay Per Click advertising, or PPC.

You simply apply for your Google Adsense account, copy and paste the code into your blog and your ads appear. As your traffic levels increase, the amount of money you can earn from your PPC ads also increases.

You don't have to limit yourself to Google Adsense if you don't want to. There are plenty of other PPC advertising options available for you to choose from.

These include:

- Yahoo! Contextual Ads (http://contextualads.yahoo.net/),
- Chitika (www.chitika.com),
- Bidvertiser (www.bidvertiser.com),
- Adbrite (www.adbrite.com)

× Clicksor (http://www.clicksor.com/)

Take some time to compare what each ad network has to offer. Look at other bloggers' experiences with each network and see which ones are likely to suit your blog and your niche best.

Many bloggers also incorporate text-based ads. These are ads that show up as links within your content that are paid for by various advertisers. Some of those links simply point to the advertiser's website, such as the Inline Text Ads available from **LinkWorth** (http://www.linkworth.com/products/) or from **AdMedia** (http://www.admedia.com/affiliate_solutions/in-text_advertising/inline_text_ads/).

Kontera Ads (http://kontera.com/publishers-sign-up.html) were once a very popular choice for many bloggers. These were ads that appeared like links within your text anchored to specific keywords. When you hovered your

mouse over the text link, a small banner window would open showing you the whole ad. Kontera was recently acquired by Amobee, so it's anticipated

Companies like **Matomy SEO Media Group Text Link Ads** (https://www.matomyseo.com/r/publishers) list your blog or website as available to potential advertisers. Those advertisers pay a flat rate to have their link displayed on your blog, so your earnings aren't dependent on how many clicks they receive or how many page impressions you generate.

There are plenty of other monetization options available for your blog. The key to maximizing your earnings is to match your ad options with your blog's niche.

AFFILIATE MARKETING

Imagine placing a banner somewhere on your blog promoting a product that you get paid for every time one of your blog's visitors buys it. This type of promotion is known as affiliate marketing and it's been a huge source of income for thousands of bloggers for more than a decade.

Essentially, the product owner pays you a referral fee for sending your visitors over to purchase the item. You get a commission for referring a buyer and the product owner gets another sale. Everyone wins.

Your job as an affiliate marketer is to direct your traffic to the affiliate's site in the hope of them buying something. Whenever a purchase

is made from one of your referral links, you get paid.

There are so many different affiliate networks to choose from that it can be challenging to know where to start. Perhaps the most well-known affiliate marketplace in the world is **Amazon Associates** (https://affiliate-program.amazon.com/).

You can choose from more than a million products to promote on Amazon, from electronics and digital gadgets, to household goods and furnishings, fashion, jewelry, games, books, music, movies and much more. Whenever someone you referred buys a product, you earn an affiliate commission payment.

There are plenty of other large, reputable affiliate networks available too. Sites like **Commission Junction** (www.cj.com) allow you to choose from a wide range of advertisers to match your chosen niche. The advertisers

make banners and links available that you can place on your blog to promote their products. The benefit of using a large affiliate network is that you can promote multiple products and your affiliate commissions mount up and are paid by the network as one payment, rather than receiving several smaller checks.

Clickbank (www.clickbank.com) is an affiliate network with a difference. Merchants on Clickbank are only allowed to sell digital products, such as ebooks or software programs. Selling digital affiliate products means your visitors can download the ebook or software they want right now, without waiting for a physical product to be shipped out to them. In some cases, this can actually increase your affiliate commissions, as your visitors get the instant gratification of receiving their purchase right away.

You'll find lots of other big affiliate networks to choose from too. These include:

- LinkShare (www.linkshare.com)
- ShareASale (www.shareasale.com)
- ClixGalore (www.clixgalore.com)
- Neverblue (www.neverblue.com)

Every affiliate network will have a different range of products and merchants for you to choose from. Take your time and look at the options available from various affiliate networks. Research what other site owners within your niche are promoting and look for which affiliate networks offer similar products.

Then mix and match a few pertinent products that closely match your target audience's preferences. You should start to see affiliate sales coming in very quickly if you've gotten your mix right.

SELL ADVERTISING

Many popular blogs can command huge fees for selling advertising space in their side-bars. For newer blogs that don't have a big audience yet, it's possible to sell ad space to help increase your revenue while your site grows.

An easy way to let potential advertisers know you're accepting private ads is to create a small text-box widget in your blog's side-bar. Make sure it shows up with some text inside the box that says something like "Advertise Your Site Here" or "Your Banner Could Be Here".

Link that text box to a page within your site that displays your advertising rates. The point is to make it obvious to potential advertisers that you accept private ads and let them know what you charge for each banner displayed on your site.

You have full control over which advertisers are shown on your sites and where they're placed. As your site grows in popularity you can also increase your advertising rates, which boosts your online earnings further.

MEMBERSHIP SITES

Many website owners offer lots of useful free content for their readers. However, it is possible to charge a fee for readers to access premium content.

In order to make money from your premium content, you can charge a membership fee to users.

The premium content you make available to members might include things like:

- Live seminars or webinars
- Member-only forums offering help and support to your members
- Chat rooms for members to interact with you and with each other
- Video courses

- Downloads, including reports, books or courses

The biggest benefit to running a membership site is that you can add a significant amount of recurring revenue to your online business without too much additional effort.

Think about this: imagine if you charge $20 per month for access to your membership site and you have 50 members. That's $1,000 per month revenue coming into your online business.

Recurring monthly membership payments can be set up via Paypal (www.paypal.com) so your members have their fees debited automatically until they're ready to leave the site.

If you want to offer an affiliate program to people referring new members to your site, you could choose to set up your recurring

membership payments through **Clickbank** (www.clickbank.com).

BUYING AND
SELLING WEBSITES

Flipping websites can be an extremely profitable way to earn income online. If you've built up a website or blog that is well-monetized, has some good content on it and is receiving traffic, you might be able to sell it for a profit.

The idea behind flipping websites is to design and build a good website that is likely to generate interest from a buyer within a particular niche. The site needs to contain some keyword-optimized content, a domain name that is relevant to the niche and optimized for SEO, and at least some traffic coming to it. You also need to ensure that your monetization options are set up and in place so they're ready to go for the site's new owner.

There are several ways to profit from flipping websites. These include options like:

1 Revamp Existing Websites

Buy a poorly-performing website at a cheap price and revamp it. Upgrade the design and freshen up the content. Add some better performing monetization programs and put it back on the market for a profit. One of the key benefits of revamping existing websites is that you can trade on the value of an existing domain name. Many search engines place value on a domain name that has been registered over the long term, as compared to a brand new domain name.

2 Outsource the Process

If you're not particularly good with website design or content creation, you have a multitude of options open to you. Sites like **Fiverr** (www.fiverr.com) are excellent for outsourcing many of your design and content

needs. There are thousands of people on Fiverr willing to do the work you want for five bucks.

Pay someone five bucks to create a customized WordPress design. Pay someone else five bucks to create some content for your site. There are people on the site willing to set up your WordPress platform for you, if you really want everything done.

3 Generate Traffic and Revenue

Regardless of which option you chose to build your website in the first place, it's important you find some ways to generate traffic to the site before it's listed for sale. Create a simple Facebook page or Twitter account for the site and start gathering some followers. Tweak the SEO until you start seeing traffic from search engines. Search for monetization programs

that convert well for your chosen niche and integrate them into your sites.

As a basic rule of thumb, whatever monthly revenue your website is churning, you can expect to sell it for approximately 10 times that monthly average revenue amount. Aside from making it easy for you to profit from your efforts, you have the added bonus of earning some income from the site before it sells.

4   Selling Websites for Profit

Once you've set up your website or blog, you can list it as being available for sale. If you get your design, content, traffic generation and monetization options right, it's possible to command a healthy profit for your efforts.

Auction sites like **Flippa** (www.flippa.com) are great for listing a website for sale. Take a careful look at some of the sites listed for sale and compare those with the end result of your

own site. Look at the prices people are paying and get to know what inclusions or factors increase the prices.

Look closely at each listing and see how others present their sites for sale. Understand what information or statistics you need to include in your own listings in order to draw attention to your own site's listing.

There are plenty of people out there willing to pay good money for an established website, so offer good value and you should see good profits in return.

E-MAIL MARKETING

Email marketing can be incredibly lucrative. If you set up your campaigns correctly, it's even possible to run each of your email marketing campaigns on auto-pilot.

The key to success with email marketing is to get people to join your mailing list. You can add a simple opt-in form on your website to encourage people to sign up to your mailing list.

Have you ever heard the saying 'the money's in the list'? It's true. People who subscribe to your mailing list are already interested in your niche or product. You have the opportunity to keep in contact with them via email.

Your biggest challenge is getting people to subscribe to your list in the first place. You can include incentives to get more people to join. For example, you might offer a free report in return for them joining your list. You might offer a series of free tips emailed to your list after they've joined up. You might simply put together an informative newsletter that will keep people on your list to learn more about what you offer.

Once people join your list, you need to work out ways to monetize your emails. If you're writing a newsletter or a series of email tips, you can add affiliate links to recommended products and earn some commissions on any sales you refer.

Some newsletters charge a fee for other businesses to place small 'sponsored' ads within the content. Your sponsors can choose to add a short paragraph of sales copy or a small banner that links to their own website and you charge a fee for the advertising space.

As your mailing list gets bigger, you can sell 'solo ads'. These are ads paid for by other businesses that you send out to your list to promote their services. It's important that you make it clear to your subscribers that they're receiving a solo message from your sponsors. It's also a good idea not to release solo ads too regularly, or you risk people unsubscribing.

Of course, you can't simply send out mass emails from your own email program, as that's a sure way to get accused of spamming people. Instead, consider using a professional email service to manage your list and send your mass emails.

There are some excellent email services available, including **Aweber** (www.aweber.com), **GetResponse** (www.getresponse.com), **MailChimp** (www.mailchimp.com) and **iContact** (www.icontact.com).

Each of these email services allows you to manage your mailing lists directly from your account. You can schedule emails to be sent out at specific times or to specific groups. Some of them even offer very easy 'drag and drop' formatting so you can create a professional-looking email newsletter quickly and easily without having to hire a designer.

INFORMATION PRODUCTS

Information products can be incredibly profitable. In fact, they've often been touted as being the most profitable product to sell online. If you do it right, information products are capable of generating true passive income for years to come after you've completed the initial work.

An information product is a book, ebook, report, course, audio or video that offers the customer valuable information they need. All you need to do is offer them that information. Even in tough economic times, people are always hungry for information, so there's always plenty of profit to be made.

Let's face it, when someone does a simple search on any search engine, the result they want is information. They want to learn the answer to a pressing question. They want a

solution to a particular problem they're experiencing. They want to know how to do something they haven't been able to do.

We all have enough knowledge to create hundreds of information products. Even the simplest things you know how to do are in high demand with other people. Just because you think something is easy to do, there will always be people out there willing to learn how to do it too.

Think about it. Have you ever had friends ask you for advice or help on how to do something? Do you have a hobby that you're really good at? Do you find it easy to do certain things that most people wouldn't have a clue how to begin with?

If you answered yes to any of those questions you have enough knowledge to create your own information products.

The real benefit of creating and selling your own information products is that they are extremely cost-effective. If you create the product yourself, your only cost is your time. If you outsource the creation process, you only pay for that service once.

The completed product can be saved and stored as a digital product, which means your customers can download copies of the file after they've purchased. Lots of people prefer to download the information they want right now, as it means they're getting the product without having to wait for shipping times. They benefit from instant gratification and you benefit from an instant sale.

Selling Your Information Products

Once your information product is completed, you need to find a way to get paid for it. **Paypal** (www.paypal.com) is perhaps the easiest and most direct option. There is an option within your Paypal Business account that lets you create simple "Buy Now" buttons you can put on your site beneath your product's image. People click on the button and they're taken to a payment page where their payment is processed.

When the payment is cleared, they're taken back to a page on your site where they can download your product immediately.

When the sales process is in place, you need to let people know about your product. You can create a sales page on your own website and direct people to it. You can place your cover

image in the sidebar of other pages within your site to let people know about it. You can promote it via social media or in your email signature line. Just spread the word about it.

Perhaps one of the most profitable ways to increase sales of your information products is to become an affiliate merchant. In a previous section of this book, we looked at affiliate marketing as a way to generate income. The object of affiliate marketing is to sell other people's products and get paid a commission for each sale you refer. In that scenario, you are the affiliate.

However, once you own your own information product you can become the merchant. Other affiliates will do all the hard work of promoting your product for you, in return for you paying them a percentage of the sale price. They spend time and effort finding new customers and driving traffic to your sales page. You pay them a percentage of the sale

generated as their affiliate commission – and you keep the rest of the profit for yourself.

Sites like **Clickbank** (www.clickbank.com) are ideal for setting up an affiliate program for your information products. They already have tens of thousands of affiliates searching their marketplace for new products to promote and they handle all the commission payments on your behalf. They also ensure you receive your own payments twice a month, so it's possible to semi-automate the entire process.

WRITE AND
PUBLISH BOOKS

Did you know there are people out there right now with no prior publishing history making millions of dollars per year by writing and publishing their own books? It's true.

A few years ago, Amazon released its Kindle ebook reading device, along with launching an e-bookstore for people to download digital books. Since that initial launch, the growth in sales has been astronomical.

People love the convenience of being able to read books on a portable e-book reading device. They can download whatever they want to read at a fraction of the price of a

printed book and have the information at hand wherever they are.

Each time someone downloads one of your books, you earn royalties. A royalty is simply your share of the sale price of the book. If the book remains available for sale for the next ten years, you still get to earn royalties on every book sold over that entire time.

The real beauty of writing and publishing your own books is that you can generate a true passive income that can last for years to come. Amazon has two royalty options. For books priced between $0.99 and $2.98 the standard royalty payment is 35% of the sale price. For books priced over $2.99 the standard royalty payment is 70%. Of course, if your book sells via one of Amazon's foreign stores, the royalty amount can change to 35% regardless of the price. It's best to read the entire royalty

section on their website for a full explanation of the differences in payment amounts. Amazon isn't the only e-bookstore available.

The Apple bookstore caters to those people who prefer to read their ebooks from their iPad or iPhone. The Kobo bookstore, Lulu bookstore and Google Play store also allow you to spread the word about your new books. Smashwords also allows authors to spread their distribution networks even further to reach a broader global audience. E-book intended for publication on one of the large platforms needs to be formatted to suit their precise requirements.

For example, Amazon's Kindle devices read .mobi files, while Kobo reads .epub files. Amazon offers a free ebook called *"Building Your Book for Kindle"* that explains their

precise formatting needs in detail to make it easy for you.

Once your e-book file is converted to .mobi format, it's easy to convert your e-book to any other file type you need using a free program called Calibre (www.calibre-ebook.com). Simply open your e-book file in Calibre and adjust the format to whatever files type you need to suit other marketplaces and publishing portals.

Once the book is written and formatted, you simply need to publish it to one or more of the major e-book stores. The benefit of publishing your books to the large e-bookstores as opposed to selling them directly from your own site is that you can leverage their massive traffic numbers for your own benefit.

Of course, you can promote them from your own site and any other venue you can think of. After all, the more people that know about your books, the more people are likely to buy them.

CREATE AND
SELL APPS

The number of people who use a smart-phone or tablet PC device is increasing every day. In order to get the most out of those mobile devices, users download the apps they want.

Lots of apps are free to download, while others might cost as little as $0.99. Some premium apps might cost a few dollars to download, depending on what you're looking for.

Most people don't have the skill or knowledge to develop an app on their own. However, it's really easy to hire a designer to create one for you based around your own idea.

Sites like Elance (www.elance.com) or Rent-a-Coder (www.rent-acoder.com) or Odesk (www.odesk.com are filled with program

designers and app developers who will happily create your new app for you.

All you need to do is come up with an idea!

Once your app is created, you have the option of selling it for a profit, or monetizing it to generate a new stream of revenue.

Flipping Apps for Profit

There are plenty of developers out there willing to sell established apps to others for a profit.

Sites like **Apptopia** (www.apptopia.com) offer a marketplace where you can buy and sell apps. The listings range anywhere from a couple of hundred dollars up into the millions, based on number of downloads and revenue already generated by the app.

The fun part about Apptopia is that you can buy a cheap app that's already been established, revamp it and sell it for a profit. If

you're clever with programming the source code, you can revamp the same basic code three or four times over to create multiple new apps that look and feel different, yet they're based on the same ground-work.

Apptopia also allows you to buy and sell templates and source code at very competitive prices. If you don't know a thing about developing apps, you could pick up a template and pay someone on Odesk or Rent-a-Coder to customize it for you to create a brand new app.

Making Money from Free Apps

There are literally thousands of apps to choose from across almost every category you can think of. In fact, it's been widely reported that many of those paid apps never make any money at all.

What you might not realize is that some of the most profitable apps are often free to download initially. There are some free apps

out there that make huge amounts of money each day.

For example, the game Candy Crush Saga is reported to earn the developers a massive $778,834 gross revenue per DAY* – and yet it's a free game to download. The simplistic 'match-3' game isn't amazingly hi-tech in terms of programming or design, but it's incredibly popular.

The game's developers make their money from $0.99 one-time in-game purchases. To the user, it's just a measly 99 cents, so they're happy to pay it. To the developer, millions of people paying just under a dollar add up to big profits. They also earn additional revenue from those annoying ads that pop up at the top or bottom of the game. In other words, they monetized their app for the greatest profit amount and then offered it to users as a free download.

Once your app is created, monetize it using sites like **Airpush** (www.airpush.com) or **RevMob** (https://monetize.revmobmobileadnetwork.com/) or Google's Admob (http://www.google.com/admob/). When your monetization methods are set up, your goal is to encourage people to download your app to boost your earnings.

* Earnings information from http://www.news.com.au/technology/gadgets/this-is-how-much-money-free-apps-actually-make/story-fn6vihic-1226825724686

OFFER FREELANCE SERVICES ONLINE

We've made some reference to outsourcing some of your needs throughout this book so far. But it's also possible for you to increase your online income by offering your own services through those same outlets.

If you have a particular skill or talent, you can easily offer your services to others for a fee. Some of the freelancing services you might be able to offer include:

- Web design
- Content writing or copywriting
- Graphic design
- Translation
- Transcription
- Virtual Assistant
- Data Entry
- Book-keeping

- Marketing
- SEO services

There are lots of people out there willing to pay you to do work for them. Your job is to let them know your services are available.

Sites like **Elance** (www.elance.com), **Odesk** (www.odesk.com), **Guru** (www.guru.com) or Freelancer (www.freelancer.com) are excellent for finding freelance jobs in a wide range of niches. In most cases, clients will post their job requirements and you can submit a bid for how much you're willing to charge to complete the job for them.

Fiverr (www.fiverr.com) can also be an excellent place to advertise your services. Many freelancers will turn their noses up at the idea of earning just five bucks to complete a job, but if you're able to finish lots of small gigs quickly, those little $5 payments add up really fast. If you're careful about your pricing and take advantage of the add-on fees and

costs, it's possible to earn great money from the site. For example, you might offer a basic service that only takes you 15 minutes to complete for your $5 gig, but you could potentially earn an extra $20 for upgrading the service to something more significant.

Google Helpouts (http://helpouts.google.com) is a site that allows you to offer help to others and share your expertise through live video. Your job is to provide real-time assistance to people who need help with a variety of topics.

CREATE OR TEACH
AN ONLINE COURSE

People are willing to pay money to learn from the comfort of their own home. An online course allows them to learn at their own pace around their own schedule.

If you have skills or knowledge that may be helpful to others, you could put together an online course designed to teach people more about your field of expertise.

There are several ways you can deliver an online course. These include:

Email Auto-responder

Perhaps the least time-intensive way to deliver an online course is to create multiple course modules that encompass the entire subject you're teaching. Each of those modules can be

entered into an email auto-responder and delivered to the course participants at scheduled intervals.

For example, you can set your auto-responder to send a welcome message to a new student immediately upon receiving verification of enrolment and payment for your course. The welcome message might explain that each module of the course will be emailed directly to the student at weekly intervals. The auto-responder can then be scheduled so that each successive module for the course is emailed automatically every 7 days until the entire course has been delivered.

The benefit of sending out your course modules via an email auto-responder is that every student can start their study whenever it suits them.

Video Courses

Video courses are immensely popular, as they allow your students to learn via visual media. Your lectures can include graphic examples to highlight the topic you're teaching. You can also add document files for students to download if there is anything they need to reference later, such as templates.

When you're creating your course, keep in mind that each module should cover a specific topic. Separate out your videos so that each lecture imparts the information you want to deliver, but don't make them so long that people struggle to retain concentration.

Udemy (www.udemy.com) is an excellent site that allows you to list your video course for potential students. Each student is able to enroll when it suits them and they can work through each module in their own time.

YOUTUBE VIDEOS

Creating your own YouTube channel and uploading your own videos can be a great way to increase exposure for any online business. You can link any videos you make directly on your website or on your social media profiles to increase the number of views each video receives.

As the number of videos you upload increases, it's likely the number of followers your channel has will also increase. You're able to add a link to your website within the description box of each video, so you should notice an increase in traffic visiting your site after a while too.

What you may not realize is that you can monetize your YouTube videos to increase your revenue.

Google owns YouTube, so they offer you the ability to add Google Adsense ads to your videos. Each time your video is viewed, a Google Adsense ad will be displayed in usually the bottom left hand corner of the viewing screen. Whenever someone clicks on one of those ads, you receive a share of the revenue.

YouTube also offers a Partner Program for channels that have amassed more than 15,000 of cumulative hours of watched video time across your entire channel in the past 90 days. Ads displayed across the Partner network are usually those that pop up and force you to watch without being able to skip the ad for a few seconds. These are paid on a Cost-Per-View basis.

If you can build up the number of people following your YouTube videos, it's very possible to generate a healthy income from your efforts that should keep rolling in month after month.

SELLING STOCK PHOTOGRAPHY

Stock photography can be a very profitable stream of income for any online business. Lots of web designers and graphic designers purchase stock photos to use in their projects, whether they're designing a new website or a book cover or just to add visual enhancement to a blog post.

Those designers purchase the rights to use those photos for a specified purpose. Each time the rights to download a photo are purchased the photographer gets paid a percentage of the sale amount.

The types of photos that sell vary enormously. Some webmasters want graphics to represent various topics. Others want high-resolution photos of places or people to use as header graphics or banners.

The amount you can earn is highly dependent on which stock photography site you choose to upload your photos to, as they all pay different percentages of the sale amount. Some sites may pay you between 15% and 45% of the sale price for each sale, while others can pay as high as 85% of the sale price.

There are lots of imagery sites getting around, but some of the more popular stock photography sites include:

- iStock (www.istockphoto.com)
- Shutterstock (www.shutterstock.com)
- Getty Images (www.gettyimages.com)
- BigStockPhoto (www.bigstockphoto.com)
- Dreamstime (www.dreamstime.com)
- Shutterpoint (www.shutterpoint.com)
- Flickr (www.flickr.com)
- Fotolia (www.fotolia.com)

If you're into photography or graphics, selling the rights to use them as stock images can generate a healthy passive income each month.

Remember, just because someone has purchased the rights to use that photo doesn't mean it becomes unavailable to anyone else. In fact, it's possible for a popular image to be downloaded thousands of times, increasing the amount you earn from each picture you upload to your account without any extra work from you.

INVEST IN STOCKS

Creating passive income is not a new idea. Believe it or not, people have been generating passive income for centuries before the internet even existed. Landlords generated passive income by charging their tenants rent. The wealthy invested in stocks that paid dividends. Unfortunately, most of the ways to generate passive income were often confined to the rich in those days.

Over the years, many people lost sight of the real idea behind investing in the stock market. They focused solely on buying stocks at a low price and trying to sell them at a higher price to make a profit.

Flipping stocks might sound like a good idea, but it's not actually investing at all. In fact, it's a form of speculative gambling that has just as much chance of losing money as it does

making a profit – if not more. No one has a crystal ball that will tell them when the price of a particular stock is going to rise or fall, so flipping stocks for profit is an activity based purely on guess-work and chance.

The alternative is to invest wisely by purchasing well-researched stocks that pay you a dividend. As a stock holder in a company, you're entitled to a share of the profits the company makes. Those shared profits are paid to you in the form of dividend payments.

If you choose solid companies that pay good dividends, such as Johnson & Johnson or Coca-Cola, or other large blue-chip companies with good histories, it's possible to generate passive income at the same time as increasing your wealth.

If your primary goal is to earn passive income, you can set your stocks to pay you a dividend payment whenever they fall due. However, if

you'd rather see your wealth growing for a few more years to come first, you might consider enrolling into the DRIP system instead.

The DRIP system – or dividend reinvestment program – can be a great way to increase the number of stocks you own without paying any more of your own money into your investment portfolio. Every time your dividend payments fall due, the company allocates a number of new stocks to you that are equivalent to your dividend payment.

Those new stocks are added to your portfolio without you having to pay any brokerage fees. The value of your portfolio increases and your stock holdings grows without costing you a cent.

The beauty of choosing to invest your profits into well-researched dividend-paying stocks is that you can switch out of the DRIP system

over to cash-paying dividend whenever it suits you.

CONCLUSION

Generating passive income really is easier now than it's ever been before. There are so many options open to you that can be combined with other alternatives to increase your total revenue.

The real key to earning passive income from your efforts is to get started. Experiment with what works and learn as much as you can about enhancing your efforts. Tweak anything that isn't performing as well as you would like and adjust your methods until you see the results you want.

Be patient and work on your passive income goals consistently. Before you know it, the income will be streaming into your account every month.

Check Out Other Books:

Investing in Gold and Silver Bullion - The Ultimate Safe Haven Investments

Nigerian Stock Market Investment: 2 Books with Bonus Content

The Dividend Millionaire: Investing for Income and Winning in the Stock Market

Economic Crisis: Surviving Global Currency Collapse - Safeguard Your Financial Future with Silver and Gold

Passionate about Stock Investing: The Quick Guide to Investing in the Stock Market

Guide to Investing in the Nigerian Stock Market

Building Wealth with Dividend Stocks in the
Nigerian Stock Market (Dividends -
Stocks Secret Weapon)

The Beginners Basic Guide to Investing in
Gold and Silver Boxed Set

Beginners Basic Guide to Stock Market
Investment Boxed Set

Precious Metals Investing For Beginners: The
Quick Guide to Platinum and Palladium

Bitcoin and Digital Currency for Beginners:
The Basic Little Guide

Child Millionaire: Stock Market Investing for Beginners - How to Build Wealth the Smart Way for Your Child - The Basic Little Guide

Taming the Tongue: The Power of Spoken Words

Christian Living: 2 Books with Bonus Content

If you would like to share this book with another person, please purchase an additional copy for each recipient. Thank you for respecting the hard work of this author.

BEGINNERS QUICK GUIDE
TO PASSIVE INCOME

Thank you for purchasing the book,
Beginners Quick Guide to Passive Income:

Learn Proven Ways to Earn Extra Income in
the Cyber World

CPSIA information can be obtained
at www.ICGtesting.com
Printed in the USA
LVOW05s2014030616

491128LV00028B/726/P

9 781505 541120